CHINESE

COOKBOOK

Traditional Food from China in 80 Recipes.

By

Yoko Rice

The trademarks that are used are without any consent, and the publication of the trademark is without permission or backing by the trademark owner. All trademarks and brands within this book are for clarifying purposes only and are owned by the owners themselves, not affiliated with this document.

Contents

Introduction

China is known as Kingdom of Cuisine. It has a kind geological climate, fixings, neighborhood customs, social practices, ethnic legacy, and a portion of the famous and valid flavors. All these things have played a significant role in the improvement of Chinese Cuisine as it is today. Chinese cooking can be easily divided into northern and Southern dishes by contrasting their flavors. The quality of South food and North cooking started to shape during the Song and Tang Dynasties. Today the Chinese food has an impact on numerous different cooking styles, especially on Asians.

The two predominant philosophies of Chinese cooking culture both had outrageous effects on the political and financial history of the country. However, it is less notable that they additionally affected the improvement of the culinary expressions in the country. The Chinese people have found the health-improving properties of many roots, spices, fungi and plants.

There were relatively few assortments of vegetables in China during old times. However, vegetables were a fundamental piece of their eating regimens. They ate different vegetables with rice. The significant vegetables during that period were soybeans and cucumbers, and the utilization of soybeans can be followed back to 1000 BC when the soybean turned into the staple grain in China. China is viewed as one of the top nations on the planet to have made wine. The wine was a beverage and was also blessed with otherworldly and social importance, reflecting social and political life and tasteful thoughts and springing up in contemporary writing. Pork is the most consumed meat in China, among different sorts like chicken, lamb, ham, duck, and so forth.

Chinese specialists found that meat was a fundamental food since it was a rich wellspring of protein. Yet, just the elite class could buy it. To fix this, a law was made that consistently, every individual living in China would get a free cup of tofu, a combination of soybean and different things like rice to give them a similar measure of nourishments as meat would. Tofu has likewise become a mainstream fixing in Western veggie dishes also.

Eating natural and good food items is currently viewed as the main point of interest in Chinese society. The healthy ingredients used in Chinese recipes make these recipes more appealing and flavorful. They cook food to an extent in which the nutritional components of food are well preserved. China is today known to be quite possibly the most wellbeing cognizant country around the world.

You will learn various recipes originated from China in this book. This book contains 80 recipes that are traditionally cooked in China. The recipe section will include breakfast, lunch, dinner, snacks, vegetarian and sweet dishes. You do not have to order from an eatery any further to eat the best Chinese food in town. You are all ready to cook with this cookbook by your side. So, start reading this amazing book now!

Chapter 1: Traditional and Famous Chinese Breakfast Recipes

Chinese breakfast is yummy. It typically comprises healthy ingredients. Following are traditional and famous breakfast recipes that Chinese people around the world love:

1.1 Chinese Fried Breakfast Sticks Recipe

Preparation Time: 40 minutes

Cooking Time: 40 minutes

Serving: 6

Ingredients:

For dough:

- Two cups of all-purpose flour
- Two teaspoons of fine sea salt
- One teaspoon of baking powder
- One teaspoon of baking soda
- Half cup of unsalted soft butter
- Two whole egg
- One tablespoon of vegetable oil
- A quarter cup of ice water
- A cup of cooking oil for frying

For serving:

- Soy milk

Instructions:

1. Take a large bowl.
2. Add the flour and sea salt, baking powder and baking soda into the bowl.
3. Mix the ingredients well and add the eggs, water and softened butter into the bowl.
4. Mix all the ingredients well to form a dough.
5. Take a large pan.
6. Add the cooking oil into the pan.
7. Make medium-sized sticks from the dough.
8. Add the sticks into the cooking oil.
9. Cook the sticks until they turn golden brown on both sides.
10. Dish out the sticks when they are done.
11. Serve the fried sticks with soy milk.
12. Your dish is ready to be served.

1.2 Chinese Jian Bing Recipe

Preparation Time: 30 minutes

Cooking Time: 20 minutes

Serving: 4

Ingredients:

- Two cups of all-purpose flour
- Two teaspoons of vegetable oil
- A pinch of salt
- Black pepper, to taste
- Two tablespoons of sesame oil
- Warm water
- One cup of chopped tofu
- Two cups of green cabbage
- One cup of chopped carrots
- Three tablespoons of soy sauce
- One tablespoon of water
- Two tablespoons of chili paste
- One teaspoon of sugar
- Two tablespoons of corn starch
- Two tablespoons of oil
- Two tablespoons of Chinese five-spice
- Chopped fresh cilantro

Instructions:

1. Take a large bowl.

2. Add the all-purpose flour, salt and vegetable oil into it.

3. Mix the ingredients well.

4. Add the warm water into the bowl and knead the dough until it turns smooth.

5. Cover the dough and set it aside.

6. Take a large frying pan.

7. Add the sesame oil into the pan and heat it well.

8. Add the chopped tofu into the pan.

9. Cook the tofu well.

10. Add the carrots and cabbage into the pan and cook well.

11. Add the pan's soy sauce, Chinese five-spice, chili paste, salt, and black pepper.

12. Add the sugar and corn starch into the pan and mix all the ingredients well.

13. Cook the vegetables and then dish out the mixture.

14. Make small round balls from the prepared dough and add the cooked mixture in between each dough.

15. Roll out the dough into a semi-thick pancake.

16. Heat the vegetable oil into the pan and cook these pancakes until they turn golden brown on both sides.

17. Dish out when the pancakes are done.

18. Garnish the pancakes with fresh chopped cilantro on top.

19. The dish is ready to be served.

1.3 Chinese Breakfast Steamed Buns Recipe

Preparation Time: 30 minutes

Cooking Time: 25 minutes

Serving: 4

Ingredients:

- Four cups of all-purpose flour
- One teaspoon of sesame seeds
- One teaspoon of oyster sauce
- One teaspoon of soy sauce
- One cup of water
- Half teaspoon of active yeast
- Half cup of sugar
- A quarter cup of cooked jackfruit

Instructions:

1. In a large bowl
2. Add the active yeast and sugar into the bowl.
3. Add the dry ingredients in a separate bowl.

4. Add the active yeast mixture into the dry ingredients.

5. Knead the dough.

6. Make small buns and place them on a baking tray.

7. Add the rest of the ingredients in a small bowl.

8. Add this mixture in between the buns and place it on the tray.

9. Steam the buns for fifteen to twenty minutes.

10.   The dish is ready to be served.

1.4 Chinese Breakfast Wonton Soup Recipe

Preparation Time: 30 minutes

Cooking Time: 10 minutes

Serving: 4

Ingredients:

- Two cups of frozen wonton
- Two tablespoons of minced garlic
- Two tablespoons of minced ginger
- Half cup of cilantro
- Two tablespoons of sesame oil
- Two tablespoons of cornflour
- Two cups of rice noodles
- Half cup of water
- Two cups of vegetable stock
- One cup of chopped tomatoes
- One teaspoon of Chinese five-spice powder
- One cup of onion
- Half teaspoon of Chinese paprika

Instructions:

1. Take a pan.

2. Add in the oil and onions.

3. Cook the onions until they become soft and fragrant.

4. Add in the chopped garlic and ginger.

5. Cook the mixture and add the tomatoes to it.

6. Add the spices and sauces.

7. Add the frozen wontons into it when the tomatoes are done.

8. Add in the vegetable broth.

9. Add the noodles.

10. Add the cornflour and the rest of the ingredients except the cilantro.

11. Mix the ingredients carefully and cover the pan.

12. Add cilantro on top.

13. Your dish is ready to be served.

1.5 Chinese Breakfast Tofu Porridge Recipe

Preparation Time: 30 minutes

Cooking Time: 30 minutes

Serving: 4

Ingredients:

- Two cups of vegetable stock
- Two tablespoons of crushed garlic and ginger
- A pinch of salt
- A teaspoon of black pepper
- Two tablespoons of sesame oil
- One cup of dried white wine
- One cup of onion
- Three tablespoons of all-purpose flour
- Two tablespoons of soy sauce
- Two cups of tofu
- One tablespoon of Chinese five-spice
- One bay leaf
- Two tablespoons of fresh chives
- One cup of coconut milk
- One cup of rice
- One cup of chopped dill

Instructions:

1. Take a large saucepan.
2. Add the oil and onions into the pan.
3. Cook the onions until they turn golden brown.
4. Add the crushed garlic and ginger into the pan.
5. Add the spices into the mixture.
6. Add the all-purpose flour, soy sauce, and dried white wine.
7. Add the vegetable stock and corn kernels.
8. Cover the pan with a lid for five minutes.
9. Let the ingredients cook perfectly.
10. Add the milk, rice, and the rest of the ingredients into the saucepan.
11. Add the chopped fresh dill on top.
12. Serve the porridge when hot.
13. The dish is ready to be served.

1.6 Chinese Breakfast Dim Sum Recipe

Preparation Time: 10 minutes

Cooking Time: 20 minutes

Serving: 4

Ingredients:

- Two tablespoons of sesame oil
- One tablespoon of red pepper flakes
- One cup of chopped beef
- Three garlic cloves
- Three diced shallots
- One bay leaf
- One lemon
- Half teaspoon of kosher salt
- One teaspoon of black pepper
- Chopped parsley
- A pack of wrappers
- One cup of oil
- Two teaspoons of miso paste

Instructions:

1. Take a saucepan and add the oil in it.

2. Heat the oil and add the chopped beef, salt, pepper in it.

3. Cook it for few minutes until beef becomes soft and translucent.

4. Add the garlic, bay leaf, and red pepper flakes in it.

5. Cook it until the mixture becomes fragrant.

6. Add the tomatoes and some water to the cooking mixture.

7. Add the lemon juice, miso paste, kosher salt, and black pepper into the cooking mixture.

8. Grind the mixture when the tomatoes are done.

9. Your beef filling is ready.

10. Take the wrappers and place the filling there and fold them carefully.

11. Add oil into a frying pan.

12. Fry the bites well until they turn light brown in color.

13. Dish out when the bites are done.

14. Garnish the dish with fresh chopped parsley.

15. Your dish is ready to be served.

1.7 Chinese Pork and Corn Noodles Recipe

Preparation Time: 30 minutes

Cooking Time: 20 minutes

Serving: 4

Ingredients:

- One tablespoon of sriracha sauce
- Half cup of chopped celery
- Half cup of boiled corn
- One teaspoon of rice wine
- One teaspoon of fresh ginger
- One tablespoon of fish sauce
- One tablespoon of soy sauce
- Half teaspoon of Chinese five-spice
- Half cup of fresh cilantro leaves
- A quarter cup of fresh basil leaves
- One cup of vegetable broth
- Two cups of pork
- One teaspoon of minced lemongrass
- One teaspoon of chopped garlic
- Two teaspoons of vegetable oil
- Two cups of rice noodles

- Half cup of water

Instructions:

1. Take a wok.
2. Add the minced lemongrass, sriracha sauce, chopped garlic, Chinese five-spice, basil leaves, and ginger into the wok.
3. Add the vegetable broth and sauces into the wok mixture.
4. Cook the dish for ten minutes.
5. Add the pork and corn into the mixture.
6. Mix the vegetables well and cook it for five minutes.
7. Cook the ingredients well and mix them with the rest of the ingredients.
8. Reduce the heat of the stove.
9. Add the rice noodles and water into the pan.
10. Add the rest of the ingredients into it.
11. Cook the dish for fifteen more minutes.
12. Pour the cilantro into the dish.
13. Mix the noodles and then dish them out.
14. Your dish is ready to be served.

1.8 Chinese Breakfast Fried Rice Recipe

Preparation Time: 30 minutes

Cooking Time: 10 minutes

Serving: 4

Ingredients:

- Two red chilies
- One large jalapeno
- Half cup of sliced green onions
- One teaspoon of white peppercorns
- One teaspoon of fresh ginger
- One tablespoon of fish sauce
- One tablespoon of soy sauce
- Half teaspoon of Chinese five-spice
- Two tablespoons of chili garlic sauce
- Half cup of fresh cilantro leaves
- A quarter of fresh basil leaves
- One cup of vegetable broth
- One teaspoon of minced lemongrass
- One teaspoon of chopped garlic
- Two tablespoons of sesame oil
- One egg

- Half cup of mixed vegetables
- Two cups of cooked brown rice

Instructions:

1. Take a wok.
2. Add the minced lemongrass, white peppercorns, chopped garlic, Chinese five-spice, red chilies, basil leaves, and ginger into the wok.
3. Add the mixed vegetables into the pan.
4. Stir-fry the mixed vegetables.
5. Add the vegetable broth and sauces into the wok mixture.
6. Cook the dish for ten minutes.
7. Add the cooked brown rice into the mixture.
8. Mix the rice well and cook it for five minutes.
9. Add the egg into the wok by pushing the rest of the ingredients aside.
10. Cook the dish for five more minutes.
11. Mix everything together.
12. Add the cilantro into the dish.
13. Mix the rice and then dish it out.
14. Your dish is ready to be served.

1.9 Chinese Steamed Vegetable and Chicken Dumpling Recipe

Preparation Time: 50 minutes

Cooking Time: 30 minutes

Serving: 4

Ingredients:

- Half cup of mixed vegetables
- One tablespoon of thin soy sauce
- Half teaspoon of cinnamon powder
- One tablespoon of sweet vinegar
- One tablespoon of Chinese five-spice powder
- Two cups of minced chicken
- Half tablespoon of fresh shallot
- One cup of milk
- One tablespoon of vegetable oil
- One cup of all-purpose flour
- Half cup of whole wheat flour
- A pinch of salt
- Half cup of chopped chives

Instructions:

1. Take a bowl and add the flour into it.

2. Add lukewarm water in it.

3. Set aside for half-hour.

4. Take the whole wheat flour.

5. Add the salt and some milk in it.

6. Combine the ingredients to form a soft dough.

7. Knee it for ten minutes.

8. Make small balls from the dough.

9. Take a small bowl.

10. Add the mixed vegetables, minced chicken, chives, and the rest of the ingredients.

11. Add the formed mixture into the round dough with the help of the oil.

12. Steam the dumplings in a water bath for ten minutes.

13. Take out the dumplings when done.

14. Your dish is ready to be served.

1.10 Chinese Wonton Noodles Recipe

Preparation Time: 30 minutes

Cooking Time: 20 minutes

Serving: 4

Ingredients:

- One tablespoon of sriracha sauce
- Half cup of chopped celery
- One teaspoon of rice wine
- One teaspoon of fresh ginger
- One tablespoon of fish sauce
- One tablespoon of soy sauce
- Half teaspoon of Chinese five-spice
- Half cup of fresh cilantro leaves
- A quarter cup of fresh basil leaves
- One cup of vegetable broth
- Two cups of frozen wontons
- One teaspoon of minced lemongrass
- One teaspoon of chopped garlic
- Two teaspoons of vegetable oil
- Two cups of rice noodles
- Half cup of water

Instructions:

1. Take a wok.
2. Add the minced lemongrass, sriracha sauce, chopped garlic, Chinese five-spice, basil leaves and ginger into the wok.
3. Add the vegetable broth and sauces into the wok mixture.
4. Cook the dish for ten minutes.
5. Add the frozen wontons into the mixture.
6. Mix the vegetables well and cook it for five minutes.
7. Cook the ingredients well and mix them with the rest of the ingredients.
8. Reduce the heat of the stove.
9. Add the rice noodles and water into the pan.
10. Add the rest of the ingredients into it.
11. Cook the dish for fifteen more minutes.
12. Add the cilantro into the dish.
13. Mix the noodles and then dish it out.
14. Your dish is ready to be served.

Chapter 2: Traditional and Famous Chinese Lunch Recipes

Classic Chinese lunch recipes are known for their flavors and fragrance all over the world. Following are some classic Chinese recipes that are rich in healthy nutrients, and you can easily make them with the detailed instructions given in each recipe:

2.1 Chinese Baked General Tso Chicken Recipe

Preparation Time: 5 minutes

Cooking Time: 20 minutes

Serving: 4

Ingredients:

- One pound of chicken pieces
- Two cups of corn flakes
- Two eggs
- Cooking spray
- Two garlic cloves
- One cup of chicken broth
- One teaspoon of sriracha sauce
- One tablespoon of Dijon mustard
- Two tablespoons of vinegar

- A pinch of salt
- A pinch of black pepper

Instructions:

1. Take a bowl.
2. Add the eggs into the bowl and mix well.
3. Dip the chicken pieces in the egg mixture and coat them with corn flakes.
4. Add the cooking spray on top and bake the chicken pieces
5. Add the rest of the ingredients into the bowl.
6. Mix well.
7. Add the rest of the ingredients into a pan and cook.
8. Cook well to get a thick and homogenized mixture.
9. Dish out the chicken pieces when done and then dump them into the prepared sauce.
10. Bake the chicken pieces again for ten minutes.
11. Your dish is ready to be served.

2.2 Chinese Chicken Egg Foo Young Recipe

Preparation Time: 20 minutes

Cooking Time: 20 minutes

Serving: 4

Ingredients:

- Half teaspoon of ground garlic
- A pinch of salt
- Two Chinese pepper
- One teaspoon of ground pepper
- Half cup of foo young sauce
- One red onion
- Cilantro as required
- Two tablespoons of sesame oil
- Half cup of tapioca flour
- Half cup of almond flour
- One cup of sliced scallion
- One cup of coconut milk
- Half teaspoon of Chinese five-spice powder
- Half teaspoon of ground ginger

Instructions:

1. Mix in both the flours in a bowl.
2. Add the chopped red onions.
3. Add the sliced scallions into the bowl.
4. Add in the spices, Chinese pepper, and cilantro.
5. Mix the ingredients carefully.
6. Grease a pan with sesame oil.
7. Add the mixture in small quantities in a pan.
8. Let the pancakes turn golden on both sides.
9. Add a little cilantro and foo young sauce on top of the pancakes.
10. You can garnish the pancakes with any other thing that you prefer.
11. Your dish is ready to be served.

2.3 Chinese Paleo Sweet and Sour Chicken Recipe

Preparation Time: 30 minutes

Cooking Time: 25 minutes

Serving: 4

Ingredients:

- Two tablespoon of rice wine
- One teaspoon of caster sugar
- A quarter teaspoon of Sichuan pepper
- Two teaspoon of chopped red chili
- Black pepper
- Salt
- One tablespoon of chopped ginger
- One tablespoon of chopped garlic
- Half cup of finely chopped spring onions
- Two tablespoon of sesame oil
- Four tablespoon of dark soy sauce
- Two cups of chicken pieces
- Two cups of pineapple
- Cooked white rice

Instructions:

1. Wash and cut the pineapple into small equally sized pieces.

2. Take a large pan.

3. Heat the oil in a pan and add the spring onions in it.

4. Cook it until they become soft and golden brown in color.

5. Add the chopped ginger and garlic into the pan.

6. Add the rice wine and chicken in the pan.

7. Cook the mixture well for about ten minutes until they are roasted.

8. Add pineapple, caster sugar, Sichuan pepper, red chili pepper, dark soy sauce, black pepper and salt into the pan.

9. Cook the ingredients well for about fifteen minutes on low heat.

10. Serve this dish with cooked white rice.

11. Your dish is ready to be served.

2.4 Chinese Sweet and Sour Beef Recipe

Preparation Time: 30 minutes

Cooking Time: 25 minutes

Serving: 4

Ingredients:

- Two tablespoon of rice wine
- One teaspoon of caster sugar
- A quarter teaspoon of Sichuan pepper
- Two teaspoon of chopped red chili
- Black pepper
- Salt
- One tablespoon of chopped ginger
- One tablespoon of chopped garlic
- Half cup of finely chopped spring onions
- Two tablespoon of sesame oil
- Four tablespoon of dark soy sauce
- Two cups of beef pieces
- Two cups of pineapple
- Cooked white rice

Instructions:

1. Wash and cut the pineapple into small equally sized pieces.

2. Take a large pan.

3. Heat the oil in a pan and add the spring onions in it.

4. Cook it until they become soft and golden brown in color.

5. Add the chopped ginger and garlic into the pan.

6. Add the rice wine and beef in the pan.

7. Cook the mixture well for about ten minutes until they are roasted.

8. Add pineapple, caster sugar, Sichuan pepper, red chili pepper, dark soy sauce, black pepper and salt into the pan.

9. Cook the ingredients well for about fifteen minutes on low heat.

10. Serve this dish with cooked white rice.

11. Your dish is ready to be served.

2.5 Chinese Slow Cooker Broccoli Beef Recipe

Preparation Time: 30 minutes

Cooking Time: 50 minutes

Serving: 4

Ingredients:

- Two tablespoons of rice wine
- One teaspoon of caster sugar
- A quarter teaspoon of Sichuan pepper
- Two teaspoons of chopped red chili
- Black pepper
- Salt
- One tablespoon of chopped ginger
- One tablespoon of chopped garlic
- Half cup of finely chopped spring onions
- Two tablespoons of sesame oil
- Four tablespoons of dark soy sauce
- Two cups of beef cubes
- Two cups of broccoli florets
- Cooked white rice

Instructions:

1. Wash and cut the broccoli into small, equally sized pieces.
2. Take a large pan.
3. Heat the oil in a pan and add the spring onions in it.
4. Cook it until they become soft and golden brown in color.
5. Add the chopped ginger and garlic into the pan.
6. Add the rice, wine, and beef in the pan.
7. Cook the mixture well for about ten minutes until they are roasted.
8. Add broccoli florets, caster sugar, Sichuan pepper, red chili pepper, dark soy sauce, black pepper and salt into the pan.
9. Cook the ingredients well for about forty minutes on low heat.
10. Serve this slow cooker dish with cooked white rice.
11. Your dish is ready to be served.

2.6 Chinese Lo Mein Noodles Recipe

Preparation Time: 30 minutes

Cooking Time: 20 minutes

Serving: 4

Ingredients:

- One tablespoon of lo mein sauce
- One tablespoon of sriracha sauce
- Half cup of chopped celery
- Half cup of sliced green onions
- One teaspoon of rice wine
- One teaspoon of fresh ginger
- One tablespoon of soy sauce
- Half teaspoon of Chinese five-spice
- Half cup of fresh cilantro leaves
- Half cup of fresh basil leaves
- One cup of vegetable broth
- Two cups of vegetables
- One teaspoon of chopped garlic
- Two tablespoons of vegetable oil
- Dry noodles

Instructions:

1. Take a wok.
2. Add the spiced into the wok.
3. Add the vegetable broth and sauces into the wok mixture.
4. Cook the dish for ten minutes.
5. Add the mixed vegetables into the mixture.
6. Mix the vegetables well and cook it for five minutes.
7. Cook the ingredients well and mix them with the rest of the ingredients.
8. Reduce the heat of the stove.
9. Add the dry noodles and water into the pan.
10. Add the rest of the ingredients into it.
11. Cook the dish for fifteen more minutes.
12. Add the cilantro into the dish.
13. Mix the noodles and then dish them out.
14. Your dish is ready to be served.

2.7 Chinese Sticky Honey Spare Ribs Recipe

Preparation Time: 5 minutes

Cooking Time: 20 minutes

Serving: 4

Ingredients:

- One pound of beef ribs
- Two eggs
- Cooking spray
- Two teaspoons of sesame seeds
- One cup of beef broth
- One teaspoon of sriracha sauce
- One tablespoon of honey
- Two tablespoons of vinegar
- A pinch of salt
- A pinch of black pepper

Instructions:

1. Take a bowl.
2. Add the eggs into the bowl and mix well.
3. Dip the beef ribs in the egg mixture.

4. Add the cooking spray on top and bake the beef ribs.

5. Add the rest of the ingredients into the bowl.

6. Mix well.

7. Add the rest of the ingredients into a pan and cook.

8. Cook well to get a thick and homogenized mixture.

9. Dish out the beef ribs when done and then dump it into the prepared sauce.

10.   Bake the beef ribs again for ten minutes.

11.   Your dish is ready to be served.

2.8 Chinese Skinny Orange Chicken Recipe

Preparation Time: 30 minutes

Cooking Time: 25 minutes

Serving: 4

Ingredients:

- Two tablespoons of rice wine
- One teaspoon of caster sugar
- A quarter teaspoon of Sichuan pepper
- Two teaspoons of chopped red chili
- Black pepper
- Salt
- One tablespoon of chopped ginger
- One tablespoon of chopped garlic
- Half cup of finely chopped spring onions
- Two tablespoons of sesame oil
- Four tablespoons of dark soy sauce
- Two cups of chicken pieces
- Two cups of orange
- Cooked white rice

Instructions:

1. Wash and cut the orange into small equally sized pieces.
2. Take a large pan.
3. Heat the oil in a pan and add the spring onions in it.
4. Cook it until they become soft and golden brown in color.
5. Add the chopped ginger and garlic into the pan.
6. Add the rice wine and chicken in the pan.
7. Cook the mixture well for about ten minutes until they are roasted.
8. Add orange, caster sugar, Sichuan pepper, red chili pepper, dark soy sauce, black pepper and salt into the pan.
9. Cook the ingredients well for about fifteen minutes on low heat.
10. Serve this dish with cooked white rice.
11. Your dish is ready to be served.

2.9 Chinese Shrimp Fried Rice Recipe

Preparation Time: 30 minutes

Cooking Time: 10 minutes

Serving: 4

Ingredients:

- Half cup of sliced green onions
- One teaspoon of white peppercorns
- One teaspoon of fresh ginger
- One tablespoon of fish sauce
- One tablespoon of soy sauce
- Half teaspoon of Chinese five-spice
- Two tablespoons of chili garlic sauce
- One cup of vegetable broth
- One teaspoon of minced lemongrass
- One teaspoon of chopped garlic
- Two teaspoons of sesame oil
- One cup of shrimps
- Cooked rice

Instructions:

1. Take a wok.

2. Add the minced lemongrass, white peppercorns, chopped garlic, Chinese five-spice, red chilies, basil leaves, and ginger into the wok.

3. Take a non-stick frying pan.

4. Add the shrimps into the pan.

5. Cook the shrimps and dish them out.

6. Add the vegetable broth and sauces into the wok mixture.

7. Cook the dish for ten minutes.

8. Add the cooked rice into the mixture.

9. Mix the rice well and cook it for five minutes.

10. Add the shrimps and then mix the rest of the ingredients into it.

11. Cook the dish for five more minutes.

12. Your dish is ready to be served.

2.10 Chinese Chicken and Broccoli Recipe

Preparation Time: 30 minutes

Cooking Time: 25 minutes

Serving: 4

Ingredients:

- Two tablespoons of rice wine
- One teaspoon of caster sugar
- A quarter teaspoon of Sichuan pepper
- Two teaspoons of chopped red chili
- Black pepper
- Salt
- One tablespoon of chopped ginger
- One tablespoon of chopped garlic
- Half cup of finely chopped spring onions
- Two tablespoons of sesame oil
- Four tablespoons of dark soy sauce
- Two cups of chicken pieces
- Two cups of broccoli florets
- Cooked white rice

Instructions:

12. Wash and cut the broccoli into small, equally sized pieces.

13. Take a large pan.

14. Heat the oil in a pan and add the spring onions in it.

15. Cook it until they become soft and golden brown in color.

16. Add the chopped ginger and garlic into the pan.

17. Add the rice, wine and chicken in the pan.

18. Cook the mixture well for about ten minutes until they are roasted.

19. Add broccoli florets, caster sugar, Sichuan pepper, red chili pepper, dark soy sauce, black pepper and salt into the pan.

20. Cook the ingredients well for about fifteen minutes on low heat.

21. Serve this dish with cooked white rice.

22. Your dish is ready to be served.

2.11 Chinese Beef with Snow Peas Recipe

Preparation Time: 30 minutes

Cooking Time: 25 minutes

Serving: 4

Ingredients:

- Two tablespoons of rice wine
- One teaspoon of caster sugar
- A quarter teaspoon of Sichuan pepper
- Two teaspoons of chopped red chili
- Black pepper
- Salt
- One tablespoon of chopped ginger
- One tablespoon of chopped garlic
- Half cup of finely chopped spring onions
- Two tablespoons of sesame oil
- Four tablespoons of dark soy sauce
- Two cups of beef cubes
- Two cups of snow peas
- Cooked white rice

Instructions:

1. Wash and cut the snow peas into small, equally sized pieces.
2. Take a large pan.
3. Heat the oil in a pan and add the spring onions in it.
4. Cook it until they become soft and golden brown in color.
5. Add the chopped ginger and garlic into the pan.
6. Add the rice, wine, and beef in the pan.
7. Cook the mixture well for about ten minutes until they are roasted.
8. Add snow peas, caster sugar, Sichuan pepper, red chili pepper, dark soy sauce, black pepper and salt into the pan.
9. Cook the ingredients well for about fifteen minutes on low heat.
10. Serve this dish with cooked white rice.
11. Your dish is ready to be served.

2.12 Chinese Chicken Lo Mein Recipe

Preparation Time: 30 minutes

Cooking Time: 20 minutes

Serving: 4

Ingredients:

- One tablespoon of lo mein sauce
- One tablespoon of sriracha sauce
- Half cup of chopped celery
- Half cup of sliced green onions
- One teaspoon of rice wine
- One teaspoon of fresh ginger
- One tablespoon of soy sauce
- Half teaspoon of Chinese five-spice
- Half cup of fresh cilantro leaves
- Half cup of fresh basil leaves
- One cup of chicken broth
- Two cups of chicken pieces
- One teaspoon of chopped garlic
- Two tablespoons of vegetable oil
- Dry noodles

Instructions:

1. Take a wok.
2. Add the spiced into the wok.
3. Add the chicken broth and sauces into the wok mixture.
4. Cook the dish for ten minutes.
5. Add the chicken pieces into the mixture.
6. Mix the chicken well and cook it for five minutes.
7. Cook the ingredients well and mix them with the rest of the ingredients.
8. Reduce the heat of the stove.
9. Add the dry noodles and water into the pan.
10. Cook the dish for fifteen more minutes.
11. Add the cilantro into the dish.
12. Mix the noodles and then dish them out.
13. Your dish is ready to be served.

2.13 Chinese Green-bean and Turkey Rice Bowl Recipe

Preparation Time: 30 minutes

Cooking Time: 10 minutes

Serving: 4

Ingredients:

- Half cup of green beans
- One teaspoon of white peppercorns
- One teaspoon of fresh ginger
- One tablespoon of fish sauce
- One tablespoon of soy sauce
- Half teaspoon of Chinese five-spice
- Two tablespoons of chili garlic sauce
- One cup of vegetable broth
- One teaspoon of minced lemongrass
- One teaspoon of chopped garlic
- Two teaspoons of sesame oil
- One cup of minced turkey
- Cooked rice

Instructions:

1. Take a wok.

2. Add the minced lemongrass, white peppercorns, chopped garlic, Chinese five-spice, red chilies, basil leaves, and ginger into the wok.

3. Take a non-stick frying pan.

4. Add the minced turkey and green beans into the pan.

5. Cook the ingredients and dish them out.

6. Add the vegetable broth and sauces into the wok mixture.

7. Cook the dish for ten minutes.

8. Add the cooked rice into the mixture.

9. Mix the rice well and cook it for five minutes.

10. Add the turkey and green beans.

11. Mix the rest of the ingredients into it.

12. Cook the dish for five more minutes.

13. Your dish is ready to be served.

2.14 Chinese Ramen and Chicken Stir Fry Recipe

Preparation Time: 30 minutes

Cooking Time: 10 minutes

Serving: 4

Ingredients:

- One teaspoon of white peppercorns
- One teaspoon of fresh ginger
- One tablespoon of fish sauce
- One tablespoon of soy sauce
- Half teaspoon of Chinese five-spice
- Two tablespoons of chili garlic sauce
- One cup of vegetable broth
- One teaspoon of minced lemongrass
- One teaspoon of chopped garlic
- Two teaspoons of sesame oil
- One cup of minced chicken
- Cooked ramen

Instructions:

1. Take a wok.

2. Add the minced lemongrass, white peppercorns, chopped garlic, Chinese five-spice, red chilies, basil leaves, and ginger into the wok.

3. Take a non-stick frying pan.

4. Add the chicken into the pan.

5. Cook the ingredients and dish them out.

6. Add the vegetable broth and sauces into the wok mixture.

7. Cook the dish for ten minutes.

8. Add the ramen and cook it for five minutes.

9. Add the chicken mixture.

10. Mix the rest of the ingredients into it.

11. Cook the dish for five more minutes.

12. Your dish is ready to be served.

2.15 Chinese Chicken Curry Recipe

Preparation Time: 20 minutes

Cooking Time: 20 minutes

Serving: 4

Ingredients:

- One tablespoon of oyster sauce
- Two Chinese chili peppers
- One tablespoon of fish sauce
- Half tablespoon of soy sauce
- Two teaspoons of minced garlic
- Three tablespoons of cooking oil
- Half cup of hot sauce
- Two cups of chicken pieces
- A pinch of salt
- Chopped fresh cilantro

Instructions:
1. Take a large pan.
2. Add the cooking oil into the pan and heat it.
3. Add the chicken pieces into the pan and stir-fry it.
4. Add the minced garlic into the pan.

5. Add the soy sauce, fish sauce, Chinese chili peppers, hot sauce, and rest of the ingredients into the mixture.

6. Cook the dish for ten minutes and add some water for curry.

7. Dish out the curry when done.

8. Garnish it with chopped fresh cilantro leaves.

9. Your dish is ready to be served.

Chapter 3: Traditional and Famous Chinese Dinner Recipes

Chinese dinner recipes are extremely healthy and loved by people everywhere in the world. Following are some classic dinner recipes that are rich in healthy nutrients, and you can easily make them with the detailed instructions listed in each recipe:

3.1 Chinese Sea Bass with Sizzled Ginger, Spring Onion and Chili Recipe

Preparation Time: 30 minutes

Cooking Time: 30 minutes

Serving: 4

Ingredients:

- Two teaspoons of rice wine
- One teaspoon of fresh ginger
- A quarter teaspoon of Sichuan pepper
- Two teaspoons of chopped red chili
- One cup of Chinese fish sauce
- Black pepper
- Salt
- One tablespoon of chopped ginger
- One teaspoon of oyster sauce

- One teaspoon of light soy sauce
- One cup of finely chopped spring onions
- Two tablespoons of sesame oil
- Four teaspoons of dark soy sauce
- Two cups of sea bass

Instructions:

1. Wash and cut the sea bass into small, equally sized pieces.
2. Take a large pan.
3. Heat the oil in a pan and add the sea bass in it.
4. Cook it until they become crispy and golden brown in color.
5. Add the chopped ginger into the pan.
6. Add the rice wine in the pan.
7. Cook the mixture well for about ten minutes until they are roasted.
8. Add caster sugar, Sichuan pepper, red chili pepper, dark soy sauce, oyster sauce, light soy sauce, black pepper and salt into the pan.
9. Add the Chinese fish sauce into the mixture.
10. Cook the ingredients well for about fifteen minutes.
11. Your dish is ready to be served.

3.2 Chinese Poached Chicken with Rice Recipe

Preparation Time: 30 minutes

Cooking Time: 25 minutes

Serving: 4

Ingredients:

- One cup of onion
- One cup of chicken broth
- Half teaspoon of smoked paprika
- Two tablespoons of sesame oil
- A pinch of salt
- A pinch of black pepper
- One pound of chicken pieces
- Two tablespoons of minced garlic
- Half cup of dry white wine
- Half cup of lemon juice
- Half cup of cilantro
- One cup of white rice

Instructions:

1. Take a large pan.
2. Add the sesame oil and onion slices into it.

3. Fry the onion slices.

4. Add the garlic, rice, lemon juice, and spices into the pan.

5. Cook the rice in the spices for five to ten minutes.

6. Add the rest of the ingredients into the mixture.

7. Cook the mixture until it starts boiling.

8. Bring the heat to low and cover the pan with a lid.

9. After ten minutes, remove the lid.

10. Add the chicken pieces in water and boil it well.

11. Add the chicken pieces in the rice.

12. Your dish is ready to be served.

3.3 Chinese Stir-Fried Chili Beef Recipe

Preparation Time: 30 minutes

Cooking Time: 10 minutes

Serving: 4

Ingredients:

- One teaspoon of white peppercorns
- One teaspoon of fresh ginger
- One tablespoon of fish sauce
- One tablespoon of soy sauce
- Half teaspoon of Chinese five-spice
- Two tablespoons of chili garlic sauce
- One cup of Chinese red chili
- One teaspoon of minced lemongrass
- One teaspoon of chopped garlic
- Two teaspoons of sesame oil
- One cup of beef chunks

Instructions:

1. Take a wok.
2. Add the minced lemongrass, white peppercorns, chopped garlic, Chinese five-spice, red chilies, basil leaves and ginger into the wok.

3. Take a non-stick frying pan.

4. Add the beef into the pan.

5. Cook the ingredients and dish them out.

6. Add the vegetable broth and sauces into the wok mixture.

7. Cook the dish for ten minutes.

8. Add the beef and cook it for five minutes.

9. Mix the rest of the ingredients into it.

10. Cook the dish for five more minutes.

11. Your dish is ready to be served.

3.4 Chinese Soy and Spinach Stir-Fry Recipe

Preparation Time: 30 minutes

Cooking Time: 30 minutes

Serving: 4

Ingredients:

- Two teaspoons of rice wine
- One cup of soy
- A quarter teaspoon of Sichuan pepper
- Two teaspoons of chopped red chili
- One cup of chili garlic sauce
- Black pepper
- Salt
- One tablespoon of chopped ginger
- One tablespoon of chopped garlic
- Two tablespoons of sesame oil
- Four teaspoons of dark soy sauce
- Two cups of spinach

Instructions:

1. Take a large pan.
2. Heat the oil in a pan.

3. Add the chopped ginger and garlic into the pan.

4. Add the rice, wine and soy in the pan.

5. Cook the mixture well for about ten minutes until they are roasted.

6. Add spinach, caster sugar, Sichuan pepper, red chili pepper, dark soy sauce, black pepper and salt into the pan.

7. Add the chili garlic sauce into the mixture.

8. Cook the ingredients well for about fifteen minutes.

9. Your dish is ready to be served.

3.5 Chinese Black Beans and Peppers Recipe

Preparation Time: 10 minutes

Cooking Time: 30 minutes

Serving: 4

Ingredients:

- One tablespoon of cooking oil
- One teaspoon of Shaoxing wine
- One tablespoon of light soy sauce
- One teaspoon of oyster sauce
- Two tablespoons of dark soy sauce
- Two cups of bell pepper
- Two tablespoons of cornflour
- One teaspoon of grated ginger
- One teaspoon of grated garlic
- Half teaspoon of sugar
- Half cup of chopped spring onion
- A quarter cup of red onion
- Two teaspoons of red chili pepper
- Salt
- Crushed black pepper
- Two cups of black beans

Instructions:

1. Take a large pan.
2. Add the cooking oil, red onion, garlic, and ginger into the pan.
3. Add the black beans and bell pepper into the pan.
4. Cook the beans well, and then add the oyster sauce, light soy sauce, and dark soy sauce into the pan.
5. Cook the ingredients well for about ten minutes.
6. Add the cornflour, sugar, red chili pepper, salt, crushed black pepper, and Shaoxing wine into the pan.
7. Cook all the ingredients well.
8. Garnish the dish with chopped spring onion.
9. Your dish is ready to be served.

3.6 Chinese Stir-Fried Rice with Cabbage and Bacon Recipe

Preparation Time: 30 minutes

Cooking Time: 10 minutes

Serving: 4

Ingredients:

- One cup of sliced cabbage
- One teaspoon of white peppercorns
- One teaspoon of fresh ginger
- One tablespoon of fish sauce
- One tablespoon of soy sauce
- Half teaspoon of Chinese five-spice
- Two tablespoons of chili garlic sauce
- One cup of vegetable broth
- One teaspoon of minced lemongrass
- One teaspoon of chopped garlic
- Two teaspoons of sesame oil
- One cup of chopped bacon
- Cooked rice

Instructions:

1. Take a wok.

2. Add the minced lemongrass, white peppercorns, chopped garlic, Chinese five-spice, red chilies, basil leaves, and ginger into the wok.

3. Take a non-stick frying pan.

4. Add the bacon and cabbage into the pan.

5. Cook the ingredients and dish them out.

6. Add the vegetable broth and sauces into the wok mixture.

7. Cook the dish for ten minutes.

8. Add the cooked rice into the mixture.

9. Mix the rice well and cook it for five minutes.

10. Add the bacon mixture and then mix the rest of the ingredients into it.

11. Cook the dish for five more minutes.

12. Your dish is ready to be served.

3.7 Chinese Easy Garlic Green Beans Recipe

Preparation Time: 20 minutes

Cooking Time: 20 minutes

Serving: 4

Ingredients:

- One tablespoon of oyster sauce
- Two Chinese chili peppers
- Half tablespoon of soy sauce
- Two teaspoons of minced garlic
- Three tablespoons of cooking oil
- Two cups of green beans
- A pinch of salt
- Chopped fresh cilantro

Instructions:

1. Take a large pan.
2. Add the cooking oil into the pan and heat it.
3. Add the green beans into the pan and stir-fry it.
4. Add the minced garlic into the pan.
5. Add the soy sauce, Chinese chili peppers, and the rest of the ingredients into the mixture.

6. Cook the dish for ten minutes.
7. Garnish it with chopped fresh cilantro leaves.
8. Your dish is ready to be served.

3.8 Chinese Poached Fish with Ginger and Sesame Broth Recipe

Preparation Time: 30 minutes

Cooking Time: 25 minutes

Serving: 4

Ingredients:

- One cup of onion
- One cup of fish broth
- Half teaspoon of smoked paprika
- Two tablespoons of sesame oil
- A pinch of salt
- A pinch of black pepper
- One pound of fish pieces
- Two tablespoons of minced garlic
- Half cup of grated ginger
- Half cup of lemon juice
- Half cup of sesame seeds

Instructions:

1. Take a large pan.
2. Add the sesame oil and onion slices into it.

3. Fry the onion slices.

4. Add the garlic, fish, lemon juice, and spices into the pan.

5. Cook the fish in the spices for five to ten minutes.

6. Add the rest of the ingredients into the mixture.

7. Cook the mixture until it starts boiling.

8. Bring the heat to low and cover the pan with a lid.

9. After ten minutes, remove the lid.

10.   Your dish is ready to be served.

3.9 Chinese Carrot and Sugar Snap Salad Recipe

Preparation Time: 15 minutes

Cooking Time: 5 minutes

Serving: 4

Ingredients:

- Two tablespoons of sesame seeds
- One tablespoon of rice vinegar
- One teaspoon of sesame oil
- Two tablespoons of white sugar
- Salt
- Black pepper
- Two cups of carrot
- Two cups of sugar snap
- Chopped fresh cilantro

Instructions:

1. Take a skillet and add the sesame seeds into it.
2. Toast the seeds until they become golden brown and fragrant.
3. Take a bowl and add the sesame oil, vinegar, olive oil, and sugar into it.

4. Add the carrot and pepper to the bowl.

5. Add the sugar snap and mix all the ingredients well.

6. Top it with toasted sesame seeds.

7. Garnish it with chopped fresh cilantro.

8. Your dish is ready to be served.

3.10 Chinese Lentil Soup Recipe

Preparation Time: 30 minutes

Cooking Time: 10 minutes

Serving: 4

Ingredients:

- Two cups of lentils
- Two tablespoons of minced garlic
- Two tablespoons of minced ginger
- Half cup of cilantro
- Two tablespoons of sesame oil
- Two tablespoons of cornflour
- Half cup of water
- Two cups of vegetable stock
- One cup of chopped tomatoes
- One teaspoon of Chinese five-spice powder
- One cup of onion
- Half teaspoon of Chinese paprika

Instructions:

1. Take a pan.

2. Add in the oil and onions.

3. Cook the onions until they become soft and fragrant.

4. Add in the chopped garlic and ginger.

5. Cook the mixture and add the tomatoes to it.

6. Add the spices and sauces.

7. Add the lentils into it when the tomatoes are done.

8. Add in the vegetable broth.

9. Add the cornflour and the rest of the ingredients except the cilantro.

10. Mix the ingredients carefully and cover the pan.

11. Add cilantro on top.

12. Your dish is ready to be served.

3.11 Chinese Sesame Chicken Recipe

Preparation Time: 30 minutes

Cooking Time: 10 minutes

Serving: 4

Ingredients:

- One teaspoon of white peppercorns
- One teaspoon of fresh ginger
- One tablespoon of fish sauce
- One tablespoon of soy sauce
- Half teaspoon of Chinese five-spice
- Two tablespoons of chili garlic sauce
- One cup of Chinese red chili
- One teaspoon of sesame seeds
- One teaspoon of chopped garlic
- Two teaspoons of sesame oil
- One cup of chicken pieces

Instructions:

1. Take a wok.

2. Add the white peppercorns, chopped garlic, Chinese five-spice, red chilies, and ginger into the wok.

3. Take a non-stick frying pan.

4. Add the chicken into the pan.

5. Cook the ingredients and dish them out.

6. Add the sauces into the wok mixture.

7. Cook the dish for ten minutes.

8. Add the chicken and cook it for five minutes.

9. Mix the rest of the ingredients into it.

10. Cook the dish for five more minutes.

11. Your dish is ready to be served.

3.12 Chinese Beef Chow Mein Recipe

Preparation Time: 30 minutes

Cooking Time: 10 minutes

Serving: 4

Ingredients:

- Two red chilies
- Two teaspoons of chopped celery
- Half cup of sliced green onions
- One teaspoon of white peppercorns
- One teaspoon of fresh ginger
- One tablespoon of fish sauce
- One tablespoon of soy sauce
- Half teaspoon of Chinese five-spice
- Two tablespoons of chili garlic sauce
- Half cup of bamboo shoots
- Fresh cilantro leaves
- Fresh basil leaves
- Two cups of beef chunks
- One teaspoon of chopped garlic
- Two tablespoons of sesame oil
- Egg noodles

Instructions:

1. Take a wok.
2. Add the white peppercorns, chopped garlic, Chinese five-spice, red chilies, basil leaves, and ginger into the wok.
3. Add the vegetable broth and sauces into the wok mixture.
4. Cook the dish for ten minutes.
5. Add the beef into the mixture.
6. Mix the vegetables well and cook it for five minutes.
7. Reduce the heat of the stove.
8. Boil the egg noodles according to the instructions on the pack.
9. Drain the noodles when done, and then add them into the pan.
10. Add the rest of the ingredients into it.
11. Cook the dish for five more minutes.
12. Add the cilantro into the dish.
13. Your dish is ready to be served.

3.13 Chinese Five Spice Chicken Recipe

Preparation Time: 30 minutes

Cooking Time: 10 minutes

Serving: 4

Ingredients:

- One teaspoon of white peppercorns
- One teaspoon of fresh ginger
- Two tablespoons of Chinese five-spice
- One cup of Chinese red chili
- One teaspoon of chopped garlic
- Two teaspoons of sesame oil
- One cup of chicken pieces

Instructions:

1. Take a wok.
2. Add the white peppercorns, chopped garlic, Chinese five-spice, red chilies, and ginger into the wok.
3. Take a non-stick frying pan.
4. Add the chicken into the pan.
5. Cook the ingredients and dish them out.
6. Cook the dish for ten minutes.

7. Add the chicken and cook it for five minutes.

8. Mix the rest of the ingredients into it.

9. Cook the dish for five more minutes.

10.   Your dish is ready to be served.

3.14 Chinese Duck Fried Rice Recipe

Preparation Time: 30 minutes

Cooking Time: 10 minutes

Serving: 4

Ingredients:

- Half cup of sliced green onions
- One teaspoon of white peppercorns
- One teaspoon of fresh ginger
- One tablespoon of fish sauce
- One tablespoon of soy sauce
- Half teaspoon of Chinese five-spice
- Two tablespoons of chili garlic sauce
- One cup of chicken broth
- One teaspoon of minced lemongrass
- One teaspoon of chopped garlic
- Two teaspoons of sesame oil
- One cup of duck meat
- Cooked rice

Instructions:

1. Take a wok.

2. Add the minced lemongrass, white peppercorns, chopped garlic, Chinese five-spice, red chilies, basil leaves, and ginger into the wok.

3. Take a non-stick frying pan.

4. Add the duck into the pan.

5. Cook the duck and dish them out.

6. Add the chicken broth and sauces into the wok mixture.

7. Cook the dish for ten minutes.

8. Add the cooked rice into the mixture.

9. Mix the rice well and cook it for five minutes.

10. Add the duck and then mix the rest of the ingredients into it.

11. Cook the dish for five more minutes.

12. Your dish is ready to be served.

3.15 Chinese Honey and Soy Chicken Recipe

Preparation Time: 30 minutes

Cooking Time: 10 minutes

Serving: 4

Ingredients:

- Two tablespoons of honey
- One teaspoon of fresh ginger
- Two teaspoons of Chinese five-spice
- One cup of soy sauce
- One teaspoon of chopped garlic
- Two teaspoons of sesame oil
- One cup of chicken pieces

Instructions:

1. Take a wok.
2. Add the honey, chopped garlic, Chinese five-spice, soy sauce, and ginger into the wok.
3. Take a non-stick frying pan.
4. Add the chicken into the pan.
5. Cook the ingredients and dish them out.
6. Cook the dish for ten minutes.

7. Add the chicken and cook it for five minutes.

8. Mix the rest of the ingredients into it.

9. Cook the dish for five more minutes.

10.   Your dish is ready to be served.

Chapter 4: Traditional and Famous Chinese Dessert Recipes

The Chinese have been the leaders in the dessert industries. Following are some yummy dessert recipes that are rich in healthy nutrients:

4.1 Chinese Black Sesame Pudding Recipe

Preparation Time: 20 minutes

Cooking Time: 20 minutes

Serving: 4

Ingredients:

- Half cup of black sesame seeds
- Two cups of water
- One cup of coconut milk
- One teaspoon of salt
- Ten teaspoons of maple syrup

Instructions:

1. Take the cooking pot and place the sesame seeds in it.
2. Add the water into it and let it soak water for half an hour.

3. Pour off the water and drain the sesame seeds well.

4. Add the fresh water and salt into it.

5. Boil the water and simmer the sesame seeds into it well.

6. Divide the sesame seeds into the desired number of cups and add the coconut milk and maple syrup to each cup.

7. Your dish is ready to be served.

4.2 Chinese Pear Dessert Soup Recipe

Preparation Time: 30 minutes

Cooking Time: 10 minutes

Serving: 4

Ingredients:

- Two cups of sliced pears
- Two tablespoons of minced dates
- Two tablespoons of star anise
- Two tablespoons of berries
- Two cups of water
- One teaspoon of cinnamon powder
- One cup of honey

Instructions:

1. Take a pan.
2. Add all the ingredients into the pan.
3. Cook the soup for twenty minutes.
4. Your dish is ready to be served.

4.3 Chinese Sweet Potato and Ginger Dessert Soup Recipe

Preparation Time: 30 minutes

Cooking Time: 10 minutes

Serving: 4

Ingredients:

- Two cups of sliced sweet potatoes
- Two tablespoons of ginger
- Two tablespoons of minced dates
- Two tablespoons of star anise
- Two tablespoons of berries
- Two cups of water
- One teaspoon of cinnamon powder
- One cup of honey

Instructions:

1. Take a pan.
2. Add all the ingredients into the pan.
3. Cook the soup for twenty minutes.
4. Your dish is ready to be served.

4.4 Chinese Baked Coconut and Walnut Sweet Rice Cake Recipe

Preparation Time: 10 minutes

Cooking Time: 40 minutes

Serving: 4

Ingredients:

- One cup of rice flour
- A quarter teaspoon of baking soda
- A quarter teaspoon of baking powder
- A pinch of kosher salt
- Half cup of shredded coconut
- Half cup of buttermilk
- Half teaspoon of vanilla extract
- One egg
- One cup of sugar
- One cup of chopped walnuts

Instructions:

1. Take a large bowl.
2. Add the rice flour, baking soda, baking powder, coconut, walnuts, and kosher salt into the bowl.
3. Mix all the ingredients well.
4. Take another bowl.

5. Add the egg into the bowl and beat it well.

6. Add the sugar, vanilla essence, buttermilk into the beaten egg.

7. Mix everything well until it forms a homogenized mixture.

8. Add the dried ingredients into the wet ingredients and mix well.

9. Pour the cake batter into a greased baking dish.

10.   Bake the cake for thirty to forty minutes.

11.   Dish out the cake when done.

12.   Your dish is ready to be served.

4.5 Chinese Papaya Dessert Soup Recipe

Preparation Time: 30 minutes

Cooking Time: 10 minutes

Serving: 4

Ingredients:

- Two cups of sliced papaya
- Two tablespoons of minced dates
- Two tablespoons of star anise
- Two tablespoons of berries
- Two cups of water
- One teaspoon of cinnamon powder
- One cup of honey

Instructions:

1. Take a pan.
2. Add all the ingredients into the pan.
3. Cook the soup for twenty minutes.
4. Your dish is ready to be served.

4.6 Chinese Peach and Date Dessert Soup Recipe

Preparation Time: 30 minutes

Cooking Time: 10 minutes

Serving: 4

Ingredients:

- Two cups of sliced peaches
- Two cups of dates
- Two tablespoons of star anise
- Two tablespoons of berries
- Two cups of water
- One teaspoon of cinnamon powder
- One cup of honey

Instructions:

1. Take a pan.
2. Add all the ingredients into the pan.
3. Cook the soup for twenty minutes.
4. Your dish is ready to be served.

4.7 Chinese Mango Sago Recipe

Preparation Time: 30 minutes

Cooking Time: 10 minutes

Serving: 4

Ingredients:

- One pound of ripe mango chunks
- Two cups of cold water
- A pinch of salt
- One teaspoon of agar agar powder
- Two tablespoons of granulated sugar
- One cup of rock sugar
- Water, one cup

Instructions:

1. Blend the mangoes in a blender.
2. Add the salt, agar powder, sugar and mangoes into a heatable dish and steam it in a water bath for about fifteen minutes.
3. Take a saucepan.
4. Dish out the pudding from the water bath.
5. Your dish is ready to be served.

4.8 Chinese Almond Cookies Recipe

Preparation Time: 20 minutes

Cooking Time: 20 minutes

Serving: 4

Ingredients:

- Half teaspoon of nutmeg
- One teaspoon of vanilla extract
- Three and a half cup of flour
- Half cup of white sugar
- One cup of salted butter
- One tablespoon of baking powder
- One cup of sliced almonds

Instructions:

1. Take a large bowl.
2. Add the dry ingredients in a bowl.
3. Mix all the ingredients well.
4. Add the butter into the wet ingredients.
5. Add the eggs into the cookie mixture.
6. Add the almonds and the rest of the ingredients into the mixture.
7. Add the formed mixture into a piping bag.

8. Make small round cookies on a baking dish and bake the cookies.

9. The dish is ready to be served.

4.9 Chinese Egg Pudding Recipe

Preparation Time: 10 minutes

Cooking Time: 50 minutes

Serving: 4

Ingredients:

- Two cups of coconut milk
- Two egg yolks
- A tablespoon of vanilla extract
- A cup of white sugar

Instructions:

1. Take a pan.
2. Add all the ingredients into it.
3. Cook by continuously mixing until thick.
4. Refrigerate the material for one hour.
5. Your dish is ready to be served.

4.10 Chinese Porridge Dessert Recipe

Preparation Time: 30 minutes

Cooking Time: 10 minutes

Serving: 4

Ingredients:

- Two cups of oats
- Two tablespoons of minced dates
- Two tablespoons of star anise
- Two tablespoons of berries
- Two cups of milk
- One teaspoon of cinnamon powder
- Half cup of honey

Instructions:

1. Take a pan.
2. Add all the ingredients into the pan.
3. Cook the soup for twenty minutes.
4. Your dish is ready to be served.

Chapter 5: Traditional and Famous Chinese Snack Recipes

Chinese snacks are famous all around the world. Following are some fantastic Chinese snack recipes that are rich in healthy nutrients, and you can easily make them with the detailed instructions written in each recipe:

5.1 Chinese Avocado and Egg Rolls Recipe

Preparation Time: 30 minutes

Cooking Time: 10 minutes

Serving: 4

Ingredients:

- Three tablespoons of vegetable oil
- Two eggs
- One cup of Avocados
- Two tablespoons of soy sauce
- A pinch of salt
- Egg roll wrappers
- Two cups of oil

Instructions:

1. Heat the two tablespoons of oil in a skillet.

2. Add the beaten eggs and cook them while stirring.

3. Cook the egg well, and make sure you scramble it well.

4. Dish them out when done.

5. Mix the cooked eggs and the rest of the ingredients together.

6. Take the egg roll wrappers, place the filling material, and fold it in your desired shape.

7. Heat the vegetable oil in a frying pan.

8. Deep fry the rolls until they become light brown in color.

9. Dish out the rolls when done.

10.   Your dish is ready to be served.

5.2 Chinese Cream Cheese Wontons Recipe

Preparation Time: 10 minutes

Cooking Time: 20 minutes

Serving: 4

Ingredients:

- Two tablespoons of sesame oil
- One tablespoon of red pepper flakes
- One cup of cream cheese
- Three garlic cloves
- Three diced shallots
- Half teaspoon of kosher salt
- One teaspoon of black pepper
- One tablespoon of chopped parsley
- Wonton wrappers
- Oil

Instructions:

1. Take a saucepan and add the oil in it.
2. Heat the oil and add all the filling ingredients into it.
3. Cook it for few minutes.

4. Cook it until the mixture becomes fragrant.

5. Your filling is ready.

6. Take the wonton wrappers and place the filling there and fold them carefully.

7. Add oil into a frying pan.

8. Fry the wontons well until they turn light brown in color.

9. Dish out when the wontons are done.

10.   Your dish is ready to be served.

5.3 Chinese Peanut Sauce Summer Rolls Recipe

Preparation Time: 10 minutes

Cooking Time: 25 minutes

Serving: 4

Ingredients:

- Three tablespoons of vegetable oil
- Two tablespoons of peanut sauce
- Four tablespoons of pineapple juice
- One cup of cabbage
- Two tablespoons of soy sauce
- Salt to taste
- Summer roll wrappers

Instructions:

1. Heat the oil in a skillet and add the chopped mustard seeds, peanut sauce, cabbage, soy sauce, salt, and pineapple juice into it.
2. Dish out the mixture when done.
3. Take the roll wrappers and place the filling material on them and fold it in your desired shape.
4. Your dish is ready to be served.

5.4 Chinese Chicken Wonton Cups Recipe

Preparation Time: 10 minutes

Cooking Time: 20 minutes

Serving: 4

Ingredients:

- Two tablespoons of sesame oil
- One tablespoon of red pepper flakes
- One cup of chicken
- Three garlic cloves
- Three diced shallots
- Half teaspoon of kosher salt
- One teaspoon of black pepper
- One tablespoon of chopped parsley
- Wonton wrappers
- Oil

Instructions:

1. Take a saucepan and add the oil in it.
2. Heat the oil and add all the filling ingredients into it.

3. Cook it for few minutes.

4. Cook it until the mixture becomes fragrant.

5. Your filling is ready.

6. Take the wonton wrappers and place the filling there and fold them in the form of cups carefully.

7. Bake the wonton cups well until they turn light brown in color.

8. Dish out when the wontons are done.

9. Your dish is ready to be served.

5.5 Chinese Chicken Wings Recipe

Preparation Time: 5 minutes

Cooking Time: 20 minutes

Serving: 4

Ingredients:

- One pound of chicken wings
- Two eggs
- Cooking spray
- Two teaspoons of sesame seeds
- One cup of chicken broth
- One teaspoon of sriracha sauce
- Two tablespoons of vinegar
- A pinch of salt
- A pinch of black pepper

Instructions:

1. Take a bowl.
2. Add the eggs into the bowl and mix well.
3. Dip the wings in the egg mixture.
4. Add the cooking spray on top and bake the wings.
5. Add the rest of the ingredients into the bowl.
6. Mix well.
7. Add the rest of the ingredients into a pan and cook.
8. Cook well to get a thick and homogenized mixture.
9. Dish out the wings when done and then dump them into the prepared sauce.
10. Bake the beef ribs again for ten minutes.
11. Your dish is ready to be served.

5.6 Chinese Golden Syrup Dumplings Recipe

Preparation Time: 50 minutes

Cooking Time: 30 minutes

Serving: 4

Ingredients:

- Half cup of golden syrup
- One tablespoon of thin soy sauce
- Half teaspoon of cinnamon powder
- One tablespoon of sweet vinegar
- One tablespoon of Chinese five-spice powder
- Half tablespoon of fresh shallot
- One cup of milk
- One tablespoon of vegetable oil
- One cup of all-purpose flour
- Half cup of whole wheat flour
- A pinch of salt
- Half cup of chopped chives

Instructions:

1. Take a bowl and add the flour into it.
2. Add lukewarm water in it.

3. Set aside for half-hour.

4. Take the whole wheat flour.

5. Add the salt and some milk in it.

6. Combine the ingredients to form a soft dough.

7. Knee it for ten minutes.

8. Make small balls from the dough.

9. Take a small bowl.

10. Add the golden syrup, chives, and rest of the ingredients.

11. Add the formed mixture into the round dough with the help of the oil.

12. Steam the dumplings in a water bath for ten minutes.

13. Take out the dumplings when done.

14. Your dish is ready to be served.

5.7 Chinese Fried Honey Prawns Recipe

Preparation Time: 5 minutes

Cooking Time: 20 minutes

Serving: 4

Ingredients:

- One pound of prawns
- Two eggs
- Oil for cooking
- Two teaspoons of sesame seeds
- One cup of water
- One teaspoon of sriracha sauce
- One tablespoon of honey
- Two tablespoons of vinegar
- A pinch of salt
- A pinch of black pepper

Instructions:

1. Take a bowl.
2. Add the eggs into the bowl and mix well.
3. Dip the prawns in the egg mixture.
4. Fry the prawns.

5. Add the rest of the ingredients into the bowl.

6. Mix well.

7. Add the rest of the ingredients into a pan and cook.

8. Cook well to get a thick and homogenized mixture.

9. Dish out the prawns when done and then dump them into the prepared sauce.

10.   Your dish is ready to be served.

5.8 Chinese Prawn Spring Rolls Recipe

Preparation Time: 10 minutes

Cooking Time: 10 minutes

Serving: 2

Ingredients:

- Two tablespoons of canola oil
- One cup of prawns
- Two cups of chopped Chinese cabbage
- One teaspoon of ginger
- Two garlic cloves
- Half teaspoon of chili flakes
- Half teaspoon of white pepper powder
- One tablespoon of white vinegar
- Two tablespoons of soy sauce
- Two tablespoons of sesame oil
- Salt
- Spring rolls wrappers

Instructions:

1. Take a saucepan and add the oil in it.

2. Heat the oil and add the prawns, salt, and pepper in it.

3. Cook it for few minutes until prawns become soft and translucent.

4. Add the garlic, ginger, and red chili flakes in it.

5. Cook it until the mixture becomes fragrant.

6. Add the white pepper powder, sesame oil, soy sauce, and vinegar to the cooking mixture.

5. Take the spring roll wrappers, place the filling material on them, and fold it in your desired shape.

6. Heat the vegetable oil in a frying pan.

7. Deep fry the rolls until they become light brown in color.

8. Dish out the rolls when done.

9. Your dish is ready to be served.

5.9 Chinese Prawn Toast Recipe

Preparation Time: 30 minutes

Cooking Time: 10 minutes

Serving: 4

Ingredients:

- Two tablespoons of mayonnaise
- Salad leaves
- Half cup of cooked prawn mince
- Three tablespoons of mustard
- Bread slices
- One cup of tomatoes
- Two teaspoons of lemon juice
- One teaspoon of sugar

Instructions:

1. Take a large bowl.
2. Mix the mayonnaise, heavy cream, lemon juice, and sugar until it becomes a homogenous mixture in the bowl.
3. Toast the bread slices.
4. Add the salad leaves on the bread slices.
5. Add the mayonnaise mixture on top of the slices.

6. Add the prawns and tomatoes on top.
7. Drizzle the mustard on top of each slice.
8. The dish is ready to be served.

5.10 Chinese Cheese Balls Recipe

Preparation Time: 10 minutes

Cooking Time: 40 minutes

Serving: 2

Ingredients:

- Three tablespoons of bread crumbs
- One egg
- One cup of cheese
- Half teaspoon of smoked paprika
- Two tablespoons minced garlic
- Half cup of chopped celery
- Two tablespoons of sesame oil
- Salt
- Oil for frying

Instructions:

1. Take a large bowl.
2. Add everything into the bowl.
3. Mix everything well.
4. Make small round balls.
5. Fry the balls.

6. Dish out when they turn golden brown in color.
7. Your dish is ready to be served.

Chapter 6: Traditional and Famous Vegetarian Chinese Recipes

Chinese vegetarian dishes are one of a kind. A vegetarian will fall in love with these lovely dishes. Following are some amazing Chinese vegetarian recipes that are rich in healthy nutrients, and you can easily make them with the detailed instructions list in each recipe:

6.1 Chinese Cauliflower Fried Rice Recipe

Preparation Time: 30 minutes

Cooking Time: 10 minutes

Serving: 4

Ingredients:

- One cup of sliced cabbage
- One teaspoon of white peppercorns
- One teaspoon of fresh ginger
- One tablespoon of fish sauce
- One tablespoon of soy sauce
- Half teaspoon of Chinese five-spice
- Two tablespoons of chili garlic sauce
- One cup of vegetable broth
- One teaspoon of minced lemongrass

- One teaspoon of chopped garlic
- Two teaspoons of sesame oil
- One cup of cauliflower
- Cooked rice

Instructions:

1. Take a wok.
2. Add the minced lemongrass, white peppercorns, chopped garlic, Chinese five-spice, red chilies, basil leaves, and ginger into the wok.
3. Take a non-stick frying pan.
4. Add the cauliflower and cabbage into the pan.
5. Cook the ingredients and dish them out.
6. Add the vegetable broth and sauces into the wok mixture.
7. Cook the dish for ten minutes.
8. Add the cooked rice into the mixture.
9. Mix the rice well and cook it for five minutes.
10. Add the cauliflower mixture and then mix the rest of the ingredients into it.
11. Cook the dish for five more minutes.
12. Your dish is ready to be served.

6.2 Chinese Marinated Tofu Steaks with Sesame Greens Recipe

Preparation Time: 5 minutes

Cooking Time: 20 minutes

Serving: 4

Ingredients:

- One pound of tofu cubes
- Cooking spray
- Two teaspoons of sesame seeds
- One cup of vegetable broth
- One cup of mixed greens
- One teaspoon of sriracha sauce
- One tablespoon of mixed spices
- Two tablespoons of vinegar
- A pinch of salt
- A pinch of black pepper

Instructions:
1. Take a bowl.
2. Add everything into the bowl and mix well.
3. Heat a grill pan.
4. Add the cooking spray on top and grill the tofu and mixed greens.

5. Grill the ingredients for twenty minutes.

6. Your dish is ready to be served.

6.3 Chinese Pineapple Fried Rice Recipe

Preparation Time: 30 minutes

Cooking Time: 10 minutes

Serving: 4

Ingredients:

- One cup of pineapple cubes
- One teaspoon of white peppercorns
- One teaspoon of fresh ginger
- One tablespoon of fish sauce
- One tablespoon of soy sauce
- Half teaspoon of Chinese five-spice
- Two tablespoons of chili garlic sauce
- One cup of vegetable broth
- One teaspoon of minced lemongrass
- One teaspoon of chopped garlic
- Two teaspoons of sesame oil
- Cooked rice

Instructions:

1. Take a wok.

2. Add the minced lemongrass, white peppercorns, chopped garlic, Chinese five-spice, red chilies, basil leaves, and ginger into the wok.

3. Take a non-stick frying pan.

4. Add the pineapple cubes into the pan.

5. Cook the ingredients and dish them out.

6. Add the vegetable broth and sauces into the wok mixture.

7. Cook the dish for ten minutes.

8. Add the cooked rice into the mixture.

9. Mix the rice well and cook it for five minutes.

10. Add the pineapple mixture and then mix the rest of the ingredients into it.

11. Cook the dish for five more minutes.

12. Your dish is ready to be served.

6.4 Chinese Vegetarian Gyoza with Sweet Dipping Sauce Recipe

Preparation Time: 10 minutes

Cooking Time: 30 minutes

Serving: 4

Ingredients:

- Four flatbreads
- Half cup of vegetable broth
- A quarter cup of lemon juice
- One cup of sweet dipping sauce
- Half cup of sliced red onion
- Half cup of sliced tomatoes
- One tablespoon of minced garlic
- One cup of tomato paste
- Two tablespoons of sesame oil
- One tablespoon of garlic powder
- One tablespoon of soy sauce
- Half teaspoon of ground cinnamon
- Two tablespoons of chili powder
- A pinch of sea salt
- Two cups of mixed vegetables

Instructions:

1. Take a large pan.
2. Add the sesame oil and garlic into the pan.
3. Add the tomato paste, smoked paprika, chili powder, soy sauce, and salt.
4. Add the vegetable broth, lemon juice, and vegetables into the pan.
5. Cook the ingredients well for about fifteen minutes.
6. Bake the flatbreads for about two to three minutes.
7. Cut the flatbreads in between to form a pouch structure.
8. Add the cooked mixture into the flatbread and line it with sweet dipping sauce, sliced tomatoes, and red onions.
9. Your dish is ready to be served.

6.5 Chinese Bao Buns with Sweet and Sour Sauce Recipe

Preparation Time: 30 minutes

Cooking Time: 25 minutes

Serving: 4

Ingredients:

- Four cups of all-purpose flour
- One teaspoon of sesame seeds
- One tablespoon of sweet and sour sauce
- One cup of water
- Half teaspoon of active yeast
- Half cup of sugar
- A quarter of cooked jackfruit

Instructions:

1. Take a large bowl.
2. Add the active yeast and sugar.
3. In a separate bowl, add in the dry ingredients.
4. Add the active yeast mixture into the dry ingredients.
5. Knead the dough.

6. Make small buns and place them on a baking tray.

7. Add the rest of the ingredients in a small bowl.

8. Add this mixture in between the buns and place it on the tray.

9. Bake the buns for fifteen to twenty minutes.

10.   The dish is ready to be served.

6.6 Chinese Dragon Noodles Recipe

Preparation Time: 30 minutes

Cooking Time: 20 minutes

Serving: 4

Ingredients:

- One tablespoon of dragon sauce
- One tablespoon of sriracha sauce
- Half cup of chopped celery
- Half cup of sliced green onions
- One teaspoon of rice wine
- One teaspoon of fresh ginger
- One tablespoon of soy sauce
- Half teaspoon of Chinese five-spice
- Half cup of fresh cilantro leaves
- Half cup of fresh basil leaves
- One cup of vegetable broth
- Two cups of vegetables
- One teaspoon of chopped garlic
- Two tablespoons of vegetable oil
- Dry noodles

Instructions:

1. Take a wok.
2. Add the spiced into the wok.
3. Add the vegetable broth and sauces into the wok mixture.
4. Cook the dish for ten minutes.
5. Add the mixed vegetables into the mixture.
6. Mix the vegetables well and cook it for five minutes.
7. Cook the ingredients well and mix them with the rest of the ingredients.
8. Reduce the heat of the stove.
9. Add the dry noodles and water into the pan.
10. Add the rest of the ingredients into it.
11. Cook the dish for fifteen more minutes.
12. Add the cilantro into the dish.
13. Mix the noodles and then dish them out.
14. Your dish is ready to be served.

6.7 Chinese Sweet and Sour Tofu Recipe

Preparation Time: 30 minutes

Cooking Time: 25 minutes

Serving: 4

Ingredients:

- Two tablespoon of rice wine
- One teaspoon of caster sugar
- A quarter teaspoon of Sichuan pepper
- Two teaspoon of chopped red chili
- Black pepper
- Salt
- One tablespoon of chopped ginger
- One tablespoon of chopped garlic
- Half cup of finely chopped spring onions
- Two tablespoon of sesame oil
- Four tablespoon of dark soy sauce
- Two cups of tofu
- Two cups of pineapple
- Cooked white rice

Instructions:

1. Wash and cut the pineapple into small equally sized pieces.

2. Take a large pan.

3. Heat the oil in a pan and add the spring onions in it.

4. Cook it until they become soft and golden brown in color.

5. Add the chopped ginger and garlic into the pan.

6. Add the rice wine and tofu in the pan.

7. Cook the mixture well for about ten minutes until they are roasted.

8. Add pineapple, caster sugar, Sichuan pepper, red chili pepper, dark soy sauce, black pepper and salt into the pan.

9. Cook the ingredients well for about fifteen minutes on low heat.

10. Serve this dish with cooked white rice.

11. Your dish is ready to be served.

6.8 Chinese Shirataki Noodles Recipe

Preparation Time: 30 minutes

Cooking Time: 20 minutes

Serving: 4

Ingredients:

- One tablespoon of sriracha sauce
- Half cup of chopped celery
- Half cup of shirataki sauce
- One teaspoon of rice wine
- One teaspoon of fresh ginger
- One tablespoon of fish sauce
- One tablespoon of soy sauce
- Half teaspoon of Chinese five-spice
- Half cup of fresh cilantro leaves
- A quarter cup of fresh basil leaves
- One cup of vegetable broth
- One teaspoon of minced lemongrass
- One teaspoon of chopped garlic
- Two teaspoons of vegetable oil
- Two cups of rice noodles
- Half cup of water

Instructions:

1. Take a wok.

2. Add the minced lemongrass, shirataki sauce, chopped garlic, Chinese five-spice, basil leaves, and ginger into the wok.

3. Add the vegetable broth and sauces into the wok mixture.

4. Cook the dish for ten minutes.

5. Mix the ingredients well and cook it for five minutes.

6. Cook the ingredients well and mix them with the rest of the ingredients.

7. Reduce the heat of the stove.

8. Add the rice noodles and water into the pan.

9. Add the rest of the ingredients into it.

10. Cook the dish for fifteen more minutes.

11. Add the cilantro into the dish.

12. Mix the noodles and then dish them out.

13. Your dish is ready to be served.

6.9 Chinese General Tso Cauliflower Recipe

Preparation Time: 5 minutes

Cooking Time: 20 minutes

Serving: 4

Ingredients:

- One pound of cauliflower florets
- Two cups of corn flakes
- Two eggs
- Cooking spray
- Two garlic cloves
- One cup of chicken broth
- One teaspoon of sriracha sauce
- One tablespoon of Dijon mustard
- Two tablespoons of vinegar
- A pinch of salt
- A pinch of black pepper

Instructions:
1. Take a bowl.
2. Add the eggs into the bowl and mix well.

3. Dip the cauliflower florets in the egg mixture and then coat them with corn flakes.

4. Add the cooking spray on top and bake the chicken pieces

5. Add the rest of the ingredients into the bowl.

6. Mix well.

7. Add the rest of the ingredients into a pan and cook.

8. Cook well to get a thick and homogenized mixture.

9. Dish out the cauliflower florets when done and then dump them into the prepared sauce.

10. Bake the cauliflower florets again for ten minutes.

11. Your dish is ready to be served.

6.10 Chinese Buddhas Delight Recipe

Preparation Time: 20 minutes

Cooking Time: 20 minutes

Serving: 4

Ingredients:

- One tablespoon of oyster sauce
- Two Chinese chili peppers
- One tablespoon of fish sauce
- Half tablespoon of soy sauce
- Two teaspoons of minced garlic
- Three tablespoons of cooking oil
- Half cup of hot sauce
- Two cups of mixed vegetables
- Salt as needed
- Chopped fresh cilantro for garnishing

Instructions:

1. Take a large pan.
2. Add the cooking oil into the pan and heat it.
3. Add the vegetables into the pan and stir-fry it.
4. Add the minced garlic into the pan.

5. Add the soy sauce, fish sauce, Chinese chili peppers, hot sauce, and rest of the ingredients into the mixture.

6. Cook the dish for ten minutes and add some water for curry.

7. Dish out the vegetables and garnish them with chopped fresh cilantro leaves.

8. Your dish is ready to be served.

6.11 Chinese Crispy Baked Peanut Tofu with Herb Slaw Recipe

Preparation Time: 5 minutes

Cooking Time: 20 minutes

Serving: 4

Ingredients:

- One pound of tofu cubes
- Cooking spray
- Two teaspoons of sesame seeds
- One cup of peanut sauce
- One cup of herb slaw
- One teaspoon of sriracha sauce
- One tablespoon of mixed spices
- Two tablespoons of vinegar
- A pinch of salt
- A pinch of black pepper

Instructions:

1. Take a bowl.
2. Add everything except the herb slaw into the bowl and mix well.

3. Add the cooking spray on top and bake the tofu.
4. Bake the ingredients for twenty minutes.
5. Serve the tofu with herb slaw.
6. Your dish is ready to be served.

6.12 Chinese Eggplant Recipe

Preparation Time: 30 minutes

Cooking Time: 30 minutes

Serving: 4

Ingredients:

- Two teaspoons of rice wine
- One teaspoon of caster sugar
- A quarter teaspoon of Sichuan pepper
- Two teaspoons of chopped red chili
- One cup of Chinese garlic sauce
- Black pepper
- Salt
- One tablespoon of chopped ginger
- One tablespoon of oyster sauce
- One tablespoon of light soy sauce
- Half cup of finely chopped spring onions
- Two teaspoons of sesame oil
- Four teaspoons of dark soy sauce
- Two cups of eggplant pieces

Instructions:

1. Wash and cut the eggplants into small, equally sized pieces.

2. Take a large pan.

3. Heat the oil in a pan and add the eggplant pieces in it.

4. Cook it until they become crispy and golden brown in color.

5. Add the chopped ginger into the pan.

6. Add the rice wine in the pan.

7. Cook the mixture well for about ten minutes until they are roasted.

8. Add caster sugar, Sichuan pepper, red chili pepper, dark soy sauce, oyster sauce, light soy sauce, black pepper and salt into the pan.

9. Add the Chinese garlic sauce into the mixture.

10. Cook the ingredients well for about fifteen minutes.

11. Your dish is ready to be served.

6.13 Chinese Wood Ear Mushroom Salad Recipe

Preparation Time: 15 minutes

Cooking Time: 5 minutes

Serving: 4

Ingredients:

- Two tablespoons of sesame seeds
- One tablespoon of rice vinegar
- One teaspoon of sesame oil
- Two tablespoons of white sugar
- Salt
- Black pepper
- Two cups of wood ear mushrooms
- Chopped fresh cilantro

Instructions:

1. Take a skillet and add the sesame seeds into it.
2. Toast the seeds until they become golden brown and fragrant.
3. Take a bowl and add the sesame oil, vinegar, olive oil, and sugar into it.
4. Add the mushrooms and pepper into the bowl.

5. Mix all the ingredients well.

6. Top it with toasted sesame seeds.

7. Garnish it with chopped fresh cilantro.

8. Your dish is ready to be served.

6.14 Chinese Moo Sho Vegetable Recipe

Preparation Time: 30 minutes

Cooking Time: 30 minutes

Serving: 4

Ingredients:

- Two teaspoons of rice wine
- One teaspoon of caster sugar
- A quarter teaspoon of Sichuan pepper
- Two teaspoons of chopped red chili
- Black pepper
- Salt
- One tablespoon of chopped ginger
- One tablespoon of oyster sauce
- One tablespoon of light soy sauce
- Half cup of finely chopped spring onions
- Two teaspoons of sesame oil
- Four teaspoons of dark soy sauce
- Two cups of mixed vegetables

Instructions:

1. Wash and cut the vegetables into small, equally sized pieces.

2. Take a large pan.

3. Heat the oil in a pan and add the vegetable pieces in it.

4. Cook it until they become crispy and golden brown in color.

5. Add the chopped ginger into the pan.

6. Add the rice wine in the pan.

7. Cook the mixture well for about ten minutes until they are roasted.

8. Add caster sugar, Sichuan pepper, red chili pepper, dark soy sauce, oyster sauce, light soy sauce, black pepper and salt into the pan.

9. Cook the ingredients well for about fifteen minutes.

10. Your dish is ready to be served.

6.15 Chinese Mapo Tofu Recipe

Preparation Time: 30 minutes

Cooking Time: 30 minutes

Serving: 4

Ingredients:

- Two teaspoons of rice wine
- One teaspoon of caster sugar
- A quarter teaspoon of Sichuan pepper
- Two teaspoons of chopped red chili
- Black pepper
- Salt
- One tablespoon of chopped ginger
- One tablespoon of oyster sauce
- One tablespoon of light soy sauce
- Half cup of finely chopped spring onions
- Two teaspoons of sesame oil
- Four teaspoons of dark soy sauce
- Two cups of tofu cubes

Instructions:

1. Wash and cut the tofu into small, equally sized pieces.
2. Take a large pan.
3. Heat the oil in a pan and add the tofu pieces in it.
4. Cook it until they become crispy and golden brown in color.
5. Add the chopped ginger into the pan.
6. Add the rice wine in the pan.
7. Cook the mixture well for about ten minutes until they are roasted.
8. Add caster sugar, Sichuan pepper, red chili pepper, dark soy sauce, oyster sauce, light soy sauce, black pepper and salt into the pan.
9. Cook the ingredients well for about fifteen minutes.
10. Your dish is ready to be served.

6.16 Chinese Chili Noodles Recipe

Preparation Time: 30 minutes

Cooking Time: 10 minutes

Serving: 4

Ingredients:

- One teaspoon of white peppercorns
- One teaspoon of fresh ginger
- One tablespoon of fish sauce
- One tablespoon of soy sauce
- Half teaspoon of Chinese five-spice
- Two tablespoons of chili garlic sauce
- One cup of Chinese red chili
- One teaspoon of minced lemongrass
- One teaspoon of chopped garlic
- Two teaspoons of sesame oil
- One cup of boiled egg noodles

Instructions:

1. Take a wok.

2. Add the minced lemongrass, white peppercorns, chopped garlic, Chinese five-spice, red chilies, basil leaves, and ginger into the wok.

3. Add the vegetable broth and sauces into the wok mixture.

4. Cook the dish for ten minutes.

5. Add the noodles and cook them for five minutes.

6. Mix the rest of the ingredients into it.

7. Cook the dish for five more minutes.

8. Your dish is ready to be served.

6.17 Chinese Brussel Sprout Stir-Fry Recipe

Preparation Time: 30 minutes

Cooking Time: 30 minutes

Serving: 4

Ingredients:

- Two teaspoons of rice wine
- Two cups of Brussel sprouts
- A quarter teaspoon of Sichuan pepper
- Two teaspoons of chopped red chili
- One cup of chili garlic sauce
- Black pepper
- Salt
- One tablespoon of chopped ginger
- One tablespoon of chopped garlic
- Two tablespoons of sesame oil
- Four teaspoons of dark soy sauce

Instructions:

1. Take a large pan.
2. Heat the oil in a pan.
3. Add the chopped ginger and garlic into the pan.

4. Add the rice wine and Brussel sprouts in the pan.

5. Cook the mixture well for about ten minutes until they are roasted.

6. Add caster sugar, Sichuan pepper, red chili pepper, dark soy sauce, black pepper, and salt into the pan.

7. Add the chili garlic sauce into the mixture.

8. Cook the ingredients well for about fifteen minutes.

9. Your dish is ready to be served.

6.18 Chinese Kung Pao Brussel Sprouts Recipe

Preparation Time: 30 minutes

Cooking Time: 25 minutes

Serving: 4

Ingredients:

- Two tablespoon of rice wine
- One teaspoon of caster sugar
- A quarter teaspoon of Sichuan pepper
- Two teaspoon of chopped red chili
- Black pepper
- Salt
- One tablespoon of chopped ginger
- One tablespoon of chopped garlic
- Half cup of finely chopped spring onions
- Two tablespoon of sesame oil
- Four tablespoon of dark soy sauce
- Two cups of Brussel sprouts
- Two cups of pineapple
- Cooked white rice

Instructions:

1. Wash and cut the pineapple into small equally sized pieces.

2. Take a large pan.

3. Heat the oil in a pan and add the spring onions in it.

4. Cook it until they become soft and golden brown in color.

5. Add the chopped ginger and garlic into the pan.

6. Add the rice wine and Brussel sprouts in the pan.

7. Cook the mixture well for about ten minutes until they are roasted.

8. Add pineapple, caster sugar, Sichuan pepper, red chili pepper, dark soy sauce, black pepper and salt into the pan.

9. Cook the ingredients well for about fifteen minutes on low heat.

10. Serve this dish with cooked white rice.

11. Your dish is ready to be served.

6.19 Chinese Tofu Katsu Curry Recipe

Preparation Time: 20 minutes

Cooking Time: 20 minutes

Serving: 4

Ingredients:

- One tablespoon of oyster sauce
- Two Chinese chili peppers
- One tablespoon of fish sauce
- Half tablespoon of soy sauce
- Two teaspoons of minced garlic
- Three tablespoons of cooking oil
- Half cup of hot sauce
- Two cups of tofu cubes
- One cup of cashew nuts
- Salt as needed
- Chopped fresh cilantro for garnishing

Instructions:

1. Take a large pan.
2. Add the cooking oil into the pan and heat it.
3. Add the tofu into the pan and stir-fry it.

4. Add the minced garlic into the pan.

5. Add the soy sauce, fish sauce, Chinese chili peppers, hot sauce, and rest of the ingredients into the mixture.

6. Cook the dish for ten minutes and add some water for curry.

7. Dish out the tofu curry and garnish it with chopped fresh cilantro leaves.

8. Your dish is ready to be served.

6.20 Chinese Okra Soup Recipe

Preparation Time: 30 minutes

Cooking Time: 10 minutes

Serving: 4

Ingredients:

- Two cups of okra
- Two tablespoons of minced garlic
- Two tablespoons of minced ginger
- Half cup of cilantro
- Two tablespoons of sesame oil
- Two tablespoons of cornflour
- Half cup of water
- Two cups of vegetable stock
- One cup of chopped tomatoes
- One teaspoon of Chinese five-spice powder
- One cup of onion
- Half teaspoon of Chinese paprika

Instructions:

1. Take a pan.

2. Add in the oil and onions.

3. Cook the onions until they become soft and fragrant.

4. Add in the chopped garlic and ginger.

5. Cook the mixture and add the tomatoes into it.

6. Add the spices and sauces.

7. Add the okra into it when the tomatoes are done.

8. Add in the vegetable broth.

9. Add the cornflour and the rest of the ingredients except the cilantro.

10. Mix the ingredients carefully and cover the pan.

11. Add cilantro on top.

12. Your dish is ready to be served.

Conclusion

Every area of China has its own fundamental dishes and culinary styles. However, preparing Chinese food at home does not mean having an index of forte fixings. China has an image of the kingdom of Cuisine. Health is always a top priority in China, so all the recipes that originated from this country are incredibly healthy and delicious.

This cookbook makes it easy for you to prepare your favorite Chinese recipes inside your kitchen without any stress. This cookbook incorporates 80 healthy plans that contain breakfast recipes, lunch and dinner recipes, snack recipes, dessert recipes, and vegetarian recipes that you can undoubtedly make at home very easily. So, start cooking today with this wonderful cookbook!

Printed in Great Britain
by Amazon

34213179R00089